LINDA McLEAN

Linda McLean is a Scottish playwright based in Glasgow. Her plays include the award-winning *Every Five Minutes*, *Any Given Day*, *Sex & God*, *strangers, babies*, *Shimmer*, *Riddance*, *One Good Beating*, *Thingummy Bob*, and an adaptation of Alice Munro's *The View From Castle Rock* for Stellar Quines and the EIBF.

Linda was the Creative Fellow at Edinburgh University's Institute of Advanced Studies in Humanities in 2011. She was Chair of the Playwrights' Studio, Scotland from 2008–2015, and she is an artistic associate of Magic Theatre, San Francisco.

An anthology of her work, translated into French by Sarah Vermande and Blandine Pelissiér, was published in 2015 by Actes Sud-Papiers.

**Other Titles in this Series**

Linda McLean

# GLORY ON EARTH

NICK HERN BOOKS

London

www.nickhernbooks.co.uk

**A Nick Hern Book**

*Glory On Earth* first published as a paperback original in Great Britain in 2017 by Nick Hern Books Limited, The Glasshouse, 49a Goldhawk Road, London W12 8QP

*Glory On Earth* copyright © 2017 Linda McLean

Linda McLean has asserted her right to be identified as the author of this work

Cover image: Whitespace

Designed and typeset by Nick Hern Books, London
Printed in the UK by Mimeo Ltd, Huntingdon, Cambridgeshire PE29 6XX

A CIP catalogue record for this book is available from the British Library

ISBN    978 1 84842 675 7

*Glory On Earth* was first performed at the Royal Lyceum Theatre Edinburgh on 20 May 2017, with the following cast:

| | |
|---|---|
| MARY QUEEN OF SCOTS | Rona Morison |
| JOHN KNOX | Jamie Sives |
| THE MARYS | Christina Gordon |
| | Christie Gowans |
| | Kirsty Eila McIntyre |
| | Hannah Jarrett-Scott |
| | Shannon Swan |
| | Fiona Wood |

| | |
|---|---|
| *Director* | David Greig |
| *Designer* | Karen Tennent |
| *Lighting Designer* | Simon Wilkinson |
| *Composer* | Michael John McCarthy |
| *Assistant Director* | Eve Nicol |
| *Movement* | Janice Parker |
| *Casting Director* | Laura Donnelly |
| *Deputy Stage Manager* | Claire Williamson |

## Acknowledgements

I want to thank Jane Dawson, John Laing Professor of Reformation History at the University of Edinburgh, for sharing her time, her expansive knowledge of John Knox, and her enthusiasm for her subject.

Rona Munro's gentle encouragement while I was lost in research and feeling as if I had a huge mountain to climb, was balm to my soul.

David Greig's absolute belief that we could do this is what made it possible.

I'd also like to thank Eve Nicol, who is the Assistant Director everyone will be looking for, because she is thinking faster and further than anyone else in the room.

And many thanks to Fiona and Brian Gayne, who provided me with a home from home.

Thanks and love to Blandine Pelissiér and Sarah Vermande for their great skill and sisterhood.

Eternal love and thanks to John D Ferris, who smiles at me every morning.

*L.M.*

*For my mother, Margaret Maxwell,*
*who believed in me before anyone else did.*

**Characters**

MARY QUEEN OF SCOTS, *eighteen to twenty*
JOHN KNOX, *forty-eight to fifty*

*A* CHORUS *plays all the other parts*

MARYS
LORDS
JAMES
MAITLAND
BRETHREN
HUNTLY
MONTROSE
AMBASSADOR
BESS
SPY
MESSENGER
GOSSIP

*The play takes place in Scotland between 1561 and 1563*

## Note on Text

The lines given to MARY are spoken by both Mary Queen of Scots and the Chorus. These should remain fluid – and be divided up by the company as they see fit. Mary Queen of Scots can choose to join in on as many of the MARY // lines as she can justify. Similarly, the division of lines for when the Chorus play other parts is up to the company.

In general, a double slash (//) means that the Chorus or characters should speak in unison or simultaneously.

A full stop on its own line ( . ) means a lapse in time or shift of place.

(Bracketed words or phrases) are what the character might continue to say if he/she was not interrupted.

Larger/smaller text indicates volume of delivery.

An ellipsis (…) in place of a line means someone might be expected to reply and either can't or won't.

A single slash (/) marks a point of interruption.

'Uh' is a breath in. 'Huh' is a breath out.

*This text went to press before the end of rehearsals and so may differ slightly from the play as performed.*

| | |
|---|---|
| MARY | // Il était un petit navire<br>Il était un petit navire<br>Qui n'avait ja-ja-jamais navigué<br>Qui n'avait ja-ja-jamais navigué<br>ohé ohé[1] |
| MARY | Everybody knows about our death |
| MARY | // Dear God |
| MARY | That undressed |
| MARY | Un-blesst |
| MARY | Un-confesst |
| MARY | Parsimonious |
| MARY | Punishing end |
| MARY | Little warning |
| MARY | Few friends |
| MARY | Mother of God |
| MARY | It couldn't have been worse |
| MARY | Had we been cursed |
| MARY | I think we're all agreed |
| MARY | // Aye |
| MARY | // I don't |
| MARY | // ? |
| MARY | Agree |
| MARY | But it was |
| MARY | Clodhopping chopping |
| MARY | Mis-hitting bone |

1. Sixteenth-century French lullaby

| | |
|---|---|
| MARY | Muttering lips |
| MARY | // Sweet Jesus |
| MARY | Cack-handed hews |
| MARY | Lolloping head |
| MARY | Rusting axe |
| MARY | Scraping through stringy sinews |
| MARY | Mary Queen of Scots got her head sawn off |
| MARY | // Mary! |
| MARY | Now<br>How could it have been worse? |
| MARY | We might have screamed |
| MARY | // Never |
| MARY | Struggled |
| MARY | // Jesus Mary and Joseph |
| MARY | Begged |
| MARY | // Save our soul |
| MARY | Sister Queen |
| MARY | If they had dragged us to that block |
| MARY | // Fwack |
| MARY | Kicking |
| MARY | Screaming |
| MARY | Cursing |
| MARY | Or worse |
| MARY | // ? |
| MARY | Unconscious |
| MARY | Our horror |
| MARY | Fear |

| | |
|---|---|
| MARY | Terror |
| MARY | Incontinence |
| MARY | Would have been the story of our end |
| MARY | // God forbid |
| MARY | He did<br>I mean<br>At least we died with dignity<br>Didn't we? |
| MARY | // Aye |
| MARY | // I think // so |
| MARY | // So the leaving could have been worse |
| MARY | And everyone knows how it goes |
| MARY | // Chop |
| MARY | Stop |
| MARY | But the beginning |
| MARY | Who knows the beginning? |
| MARY | // Which one? |
| MARY | The first breath? |
| MARY | Touch? |
| MARY | Look? |
| MARY | Step? |
| MARY | Word? |
| MARY | The first berth to France and its motherless love |
| MARY | The first communion |
| MARY | The first dance |
| MARY | The first kiss as a bride |
| MARY | The moment the darling boy died |

| | |
|---|---|
| MARY | The day we came back in a haar |
| MARY | So deep and marrow-chill that we clung to the rail of the ship until the captain fired the cannon |
| MARY | // boom |
| MARY | To announce our arrival |
| KNOX | In a city made dark and dank by our cautioning Lord |
| MARY<br>KNOX | // And my heart sank<br>// And my heart sank to depths already plumbed by bloody revenge and long years of exile |
| MARY | As I walked with steady footsteps on this plank |
| KNOX | We will all be damned for sinning |
| MARY | My beginning will be my end |
| MARY | Uhhhhh |
| MARY | The first breath then |
| MARY | // Huh |
| MARY | Let's begin with that |
| MARY | In a palace |
| MARY | In Linlithgow |
| MARY | In a chamber |
| MARY | On a bed |
| MARY | // Aaaaaaaaaaa |
| MARY | Barely take the first rush of sharp December air into my chittering lungs |
| MARY | When those men |
| MARY | Always the men |

| | |
|---|---|
| MARY | Rush in with that first-to-tell-the-news privilege on their lips |
| LORD | // Dead |
| MARY | They said |
| MARY | Barely take my first breath, my first open-eyed look at the woman holding me before my heart fails |
| MARY | // Tock |
| MARY | And in the failing there is flight, a sight of the shock from above, a dove perched on the sill coos a pillow of |
| MARY | // hoo Hoo hoo |
| MARY | // hoo Hoo hoo |
| MARY | Is dead? |
| MARY | Ton Papa |
| MARY | The woman I love stiffens and falls, we are all three of us, mother, father and child, joined in a perfect trinity of still, no tick or tock, bar the rocking of the lullaby in the vein |
| MARY | // whoosh |
| MARY | // wheesh |
| MARY | // now babbie |
| LORD | Your daddy |
| LORD | Father |
| LORD | King of the castle |
| LORD | Is dead |
| MARY | They said |
| LORD | And won't be the last to lose his sons |
| LORD | But gain a daughter and see her misfortunate future pass before his eyes |

| | |
|---|---|
| MARY | // A lass |
| LORD | // A lack |
| KNOX | A monstrous thing |
| MARY | Says Knockes |
| MARY | From above I see the woman I love more than any other, being watched and prayed over |
| MARY | // Hail Mary full of grace |
| MARY | // The Lord is with thee |
| MARY | Tripping off their noble tongues |
| LORD | Give the babbie to me, one of them says |
| LORD | Give her over |
| LORD | I'll keep her safe |
| LORD | I have a son almost the same age |
| LORD | I have a palace |
| LORD | An estate |
| LORD | A treasure |
| LORD | I see her hesitate |
| LORD | I have a crown |
| LORD | An army |
| MARY | I feel my mother's fear from here in the rafters, a draught blows through the opening door |
| MARY | A conspiracy of |
| LORD | It could be done now |
| LORD | If we had the nerve |
| LORD | The steel |
| LORD | The end might serve us right well |
| LORD | And our English neighbour |

| | |
|---|---|
| LORD | // Who's with me? |
| MARY | // Who's with me? |
| MARY | This child is the blood and bone of us |
| MARY | Heart and soul of us |
| MARY | Whoever owns the child owns the purse |
| MARY | Whoever kills the child earns the curse |
| LORD | // Are you mad? |
| MARY | With grief alone which crushes my heart |
| MARY | My mama says |
| MARY | So that my limbs are weak, you all saw me fall, but my mind my mind is a separate thing, it serves me well and badly at the same time, it thinks on as regularly as if today were any other day when the difference could not be more glaring, and so this heartless mind of mine is well aware of your generous offer to care for my daughter, who has barely taken her first breath |
| MARY | // Uh |
| MARY | And yet finds herself at once fatherless and in possession of his crown |
| MARY | They bow down |
| MARY | // Your Majesty |
| MARY | Marie |
| MARY | They reach |
| MARY | They kneel |
| MARY | They offer their swords |
| MARY | Their words of fealty and admiration |
| KNOX | Incantations of worldliness trip from their tongues |
| MARY | It should have been obvious that day |

| | |
|---|---|
| MARY | How the men in this realm would betray me |
| KNOX<br>MARY | // Even then<br>// Even then |
| KNOX | At this first temptation of their valour |
| MARY | Power |
| KNOX | Pleasure |
| MARY | Will |
| MARY | Love of decoration |
| KNOX | And frill |
| KNOX<br>MARY | // They fail to stand as one<br>// They fail to stand as one |
| KNOX<br>MARY | // With God<br>// With God |
| MARY | Or the Crown |
| MARY | So we are torn asunder |
| MARY | Ripped |
| MARY | Rent |
| MARY | Split in two warring tribes |
| KNOX | As is God |
| MARY | And his brother |
| KNOX | Satan |
| MARY | But how to know the one from the other? |
| | . |
| KNOX | Oh Lord our God |
| | That day she came back in the haar, my finger was hovering over Isaiah Thirteen |
| | Other lords beside You have ruled us but we will remember<br>You only, and Your name |

|  | The tract was meant for her brother, James, trusted by the entire Reformation to deliver one message loud and clear |
|---|---|
| JAMES | We will have no Papists here |
| KNOX | Even if she brings treasure, song and dance, Renaissance romance, she does so at the beck and call of Satan |
| MARY | He visited us in France |
| MARY | While I was still in mourning |
| MARY | I recall |
| MARY | Tall |
| MARY | Broad |
| MARY | Brusque |
| MARY | Formal |
| MARY | Acquainted with the etiquette |
| MARY | And yet hardly charming |
| MARY | Either ignoring or not noticing her widow's tears |
| MARY | Her fears for her safe-keeping |
| MARY | And what of Master Knockes? |
| JAMES | I favour plain speaking |
| MARY | He cursed my mother and then she died, I would have him gone |
| JAMES | I believe with time he may be brought round |
| MARY | And protection? |
| JAMES | My sword, my word |
| MARY | Marys, let me introduce you to my brother |
| MARY | // Step |
| MARY | My mother often spoke of you with affection, if I needed direction she said I might rely upon // you |

| JAMES | // You you flatter me, Majesty |
|---|---|
| MARY | // Ss |
| MARY | Sister<br>I insist upon it |
| JAMES | Ssister then |
| MARY | Blood, my mother said, when I asked her who<br>to trust in this world where husband father<br>and son die at a moment's notice, blood, my<br>dearest heart, without blood we are pigeons<br>and doves unable to tell the difference<br>between captivity and love |
| JAMES | You have been overeducated in niceness,<br>Mary, you had best be wary of the slippery<br>tongue, on your home ground it often passes<br>for obedience or affection when in truth it is<br>no more than intention towards a prize |
| MARY | Will you scold me for my smile, brother? If<br>there is another way to express my gratitude<br>I wish you would enlighten me |
| JAMES | Land and a title sit well with // most men |
| MARY<br>KNOX | // Most men will grab first<br>// Most men will grab first |
| KNOX | Their thirst for position being their least<br>enviable mortal failing but this man was<br>a Lord of the Reformation |
| KNOX<br>MARY | // My faith in him was strong<br>// My faith in him was strong |
| MARY | Wrongly as it turns out |
| MARY | // in the end |
| MARY | His need for power |
| MARY | And obedience on every score |
| MARY | Was stronger than his allegiance to me |
| JAMES | She spoke at length with me and my secretary<br>Maitland |

| | |
|---|---|
| MAITLAND | She has strength and learning above her years |
| KNOX | My fear is she will pollute the very air we breathe with her bishops and idolatry |
| MARY | I ask only that I be allowed the mass within my private chapel, I understand the religion in Scotland is no longer mine |
| JAMES | With time she might be brought to see the truth of the Word |
| KNOX | You refused |
| MAITLAND | She is after all only eighteen |
| KNOX | You told her plainly that we follow a straight path laid down by Joshua, Isaiah and Ezekiel, and it is not negotiable as if it were fish or wine |
| MARY | But what would they say of me, brother, if I so easily substituted one Church for another? |
| LORD | Flighty |
| LORD | Fickle |
| LORD | Inconstant |
| JAMES | It is not your mission to please the people, it is to govern |
| MARY | An honour invested in me by the very God you would have me expunge, tell me truly, brother, will your God anoint me too? |
| JAMES | There is only one God |
| MARY | So I thought and I intend to stick with Him through thick and thin |
| KNOX | And so the matter is closed, she remains in France with her Satanic horde |
| JAMES | She arrives in the summer |
| KNOX | Over my dead body |
| MARY | // You gave me your word |
| KNOX | // You gave me your word |

KNOX
There is one door that must always remain closed, a woman, a Jezebel, a Delilah beckons, and we are weak as David, we are human, temptation knows everything of our weakness elsewise we might brush it aside with an airy wave, but no, the temptress will catch us off-guard, will persuade us that she knows better than the Word of the Lord, and cloak herself in glittering decoration, thereby rendering us dead forever in God's redeeming eye, you need only look outside this city to see the multitude of men who openly express their greed and contempt for godliness, and you would let them govern us again, her cousin Huntly will be waiting to embrace your Papist sister with open arms and bloodthirsty legion

MAITLAND
He waits for nothing, his man was at her in France before I arrived but your sister has no taste for civil war, she is a young bride newly widowed, but still a girl

LORD
// A lass

LORD
// A lack

JAMES
There is no going back from it now, she will accept my counsel, my secretary will be hers, your fears, my esteemed Mister Knockes, are unnecessary

KNOX
An icy sliver of shade steals around my heart, I am dragged down again to an airless hold that smothers the flow in my veins, the whip of the timekeeper bloody on my back, my chest arches out of breath

MARY
// Whoosh

MARY
// Wheesh

KNOX
Dear God, have we not been tested enough? Might we not enjoy one moment's peace on earth?

# BOOM

| | |
|---|---|
| MARY | The prow of the galleon is lit as we enter Leith |
| MARY | // Whoosh |
| MARY | // Wheesh |
| MARY | Can you see? |
| MARY | Not a thing |
| MARY | Living or dead |
| MARY | But I confess |
| MARY | // Yes? |
| MARY | Something even in the haar, the damp clinging fondness of the impenetrable mist lingers on my lips with such softness that I can almost feel her tender caress |
| MARY | // Mama |
| MARY | Consider it a blind embrace |
| MARY | A moment's grace |
| MARY | After the race between our ships and England's |
| MARY | And a watery grave |
| MARY | No time for thinking then |
| MARY | A leap of faith in a sudden wind |
| MARY | Carries us further and faster than our imagination |
| MARY | Leaving our cargo behind |
| MARY | As we slide into this magical realm |
| MARY | // Shhhh |
| MARY | // Ahhhhh |
| MARY | This dreaming place where my mother and father discovered a passion for each other and birthed me and my brothers, dead now but |

|          |                                                                                                                                                        |
|----------|--------------------------------------------------------------------------------------------------------------------------------------------------------|
|          | their spirits no less welcome protection against an enemy lying in wait                                                                                 |
| MARY     | // Are you still afraid?                                                                                                                                |
| MARY     | More than ever, but I will do everything in my power, to steer this persevering, god-fearing, courageous, rudderless people on the path towards glory   |
| MARY     | Do well, think well, give thanks to God every day, never stray from his Word                                                                            |
| MARY     | // We are His flock                                                                                                                                     |
| MARY     | We pray                                                                                                                                                 |
| MARY     | // We are His flock                                                                                                                                     |
| MARY     | And he will preserve his righteous few, in a world of strangers, sinners, lords and earls, labyrinthine familial ties, brothers, sisters, abductors, and spies |

# BOOM

|          |                                                                                      |
|----------|--------------------------------------------------------------------------------------|
| MARY     | Barely set foot on land barely hold the reins of the pony and press it on with my heels |
| MARY     | When I hear it                                                                        |
| MARY     | That mumble                                                                           |
| MARY     | Isn't she beautiful, they say                                                         |
| MARY     | These horses can't be for us // surely                                               |
| MARY     | // Surely there's been a mistake                                                     |
| MARY     | // My heart breaks                                                                    |
| MARY     | To see the lack of estate who have come to greet her                                 |
| MARY     | Keep her waiting in a shabby house in the harbour                                    |
| MARY     | It'll take us hours to get to the palace                                             |

| MARY | My dress is trailing in mud |
| MARY | Oh Lord look at that long grey hill |
| MARY | Tall girl for that short-arsed pony |
| MARY | That's all there is |
| MARY | It's not what she's used to |
| MARY | Her mother will be turning in her grave |
| MARY | // God love her |
| MARY | What must she be thinking? |
| MARY | This would never have happened |
| MARY | // in France |
| MARY | In France |
| MARY | There would have been magnificent banners |
| MARY | Triumphal processions |
| MARY | A golden litter |
| MARY | Banquets |
| MARY | Musicians |
| MARY | Trumpets |
| MARY | Poets |
| MARY | A parade of men |
| MARY | In uniform |
| MARY | Ladies in satins and silks |
| MARY | A horse dressed up like a unicorn |
| MARY | // We saw that once |
| MARY | // We did |
| MARY | Three days of feasting |
| MARY | Toasting |
| MARY | Blessings from the priests |

| | |
|---|---|
| MARY | Not this miserable rabble of ghostly poor |
| MARY | shuffling through the streets |
| MARY | to catch a glimpse |
| MARY | of a legend |

# BOOM

| | |
|---|---|
| MARY | Halfway up the hill |
| MARY | I hear it |
| MARY | That humble tone we were used to |
| LORD | Forgive us our lateness |
| LORD | You weren't expected for at least another week |
| LORD | We had planned feasting and fires all over the city |
| LORD | Much prettier ponies than the one Your Majesty graces |
| LORD | In truth we thought you were bringing your own |
| MARY | Confiscated by the English Fleet, I'm sorry to say |
| MARY | Along with our furniture and tapestries |
| MARY | We were lucky to escape with our lives |
| MARY | // Mary look |
| MARY | A crowd is coming to greet us |
| MARY | Cheering |
| MARY | Clapping |
| MARY | Bowing as we go by |
| MARY | The welcome we looked for when we first arrived |
| MARY | No knives |

| | |
|---|---|
| MARY | No spears |
| MARY | No bloodthirsty Protestants waiting to harangue us |
| MARY | The ordinary people might still love us then |
| MARY | Given time |
| MARY | And bread |
| MARY | Would it be rude to wave? |
| MARY | They're calling |
| MARY | // God be with you |
| MARY | A sign if ever I heard one |
| MARY | That they are not done with me and mine |
| MARY | // Wave then |
| MARY | Sit up |
| MARY | Straight back |
| MARY | You're never more alive than on a saddle |
| MARY | // Smile |
| MARY | I am smiling already, the heady feeling of being loved by so many revives my sorry soul, as we trip along the Canongate I slow to let a woman touch my hem |
| MARY | // Your Majesty |
| MARY | The crowd fall down |
| MARY | I wait a moment too long as her fingers rub over a small gem sewn into my dark skirt, her eyes meet mine and I know in an instant that she has no intention of theft, she has merely been beguiled by the shine, I want to peel it out of its socket and reward her with the stone, the gift she gave me was worth so much more |

# BOOM

| | |
|---|---|
| MARY | Over the drawbridge, inside the gate |
| MARY | It is not too late after all |
| MARY | The people don't hate me |
| MARY | How could they? |
| MARY | Did you see the adoration? |
| MARY | As if we were an apparition |
| MARY | Sent from Heaven to bless them |
| MARY | They're rough |
| MARY | Short |
| MARY | Coarse |
| MARY | They're wet-through |
| MARY | But they don't hate you |
| MARY | I see my mother's handprint here and here |
| MARY | These gardens might be Fontainebleau |
| MARY | Saint-Germain |
| MARY | Amboise |
| MARY | She brought me to France, brought France to me in this Holyrood Château |
| MARY | I see masquerades and dances |
| MARY | Violas |
| MARY | Oboes |
| MARY | Whispered romances |
| MARY | This empty space filled with all the grace we inherited and were schooled in |
| MARY | Here she is in every wall, ceiling, painted plaster |
| MARY | A testament to |
| MARY | // Beauty |

| | |
|---|---|
| MARY | And the future |
| MARY | We will not be sad |
| MARY | We are the Queen of Scotland |
| MARY | // And we are only eighteen |
| BRETHREN | All people that on earth do dwell |
| MARY | // Mon Dieu |
| MARY | Reformers |
| MARY | Under the window |
| MARY | Droning |
| MARY | Pitiful wailing |
| MARY | Calling it music |
| MARY | As if we don't know what they mean by these psalms |
| MARY | As if we haven't witnessed Protestants in France |
| MARY | Drowning out the mass |
| KNOX | And I say to you, brothers and sisters in Christ, It is not too late We have been tested before And at the moment we are almost done, At the very moment we believe everything we live and breathe for to be lost He will deliver us, with a mystery known only to Him He will smite our enemy with plague and pestilence, He will strike a king a queen a prince an army |
| | Now is not the moment to be cast down Now is the moment to rejoice to sing, to show the Devil's own that we are not to be so easily overcome With David's songs, what better weapon |

| | |
|---|---|
| BRETHREN | Sing to the Lord with cheerful voice<br>Him serve with fear, His praise forth tell<br>Come ye before Him and rejoice |
| MARY | Dear friends, I say |
| MARY | While we are humbled by your welcome and delighted by your melody, we wonder if you might return tomorrow and give us the joy of hearing it anew, we are alas exhausted from our journey and must bid you bonne nuit et à demain |
| MARY | // Bon Dieu |
| MARY | These Reformers have no manners |
| | . |
| MARY | // Step[2] |
| MARY | // Together |
| MARY | // Step |
| MARY | // Together |
| MARY | // Step step step |
| JAMES | Sooner or later there will be a meeting with Knockes |
| MARY | // Which one? |
| MARY | The one where he reduces us to tears? |
| MARY | Or the one where he compares us to the mad King Nero? |
| MARY | Calls our uncles enemies to God? |
| MARY | Or seems almost to like us? |
| MARY | How short that was |
| JAMES | Nevertheless it must be done |
| MARY | I would rather not |
| JAMES | You think that will stop him? |

2. Renaissance dance: pavane

| | |
|---|---|
| MAITLAND | Perhaps if he meets you |
| MARY | He hates me he scares me |
| JAMES | He has to be faced |
| MARY | Tell me, brother |
| MARY | // Step |
| MARY | How is it that everyone is so keen on a meeting with Knockes but no one knows how to dance the pavane? |
| JAMES | There isn't much call for it in Scotland |
| MARY | Maitland, take Mary's hand |
| MAITLAND | I am at your command |
| MARY | See, Mary, didn't I tell you he had charm |
| MARY | More than can be said of your brother |
| MARY | // Step |
| MARY | // Together |
| MARY | // Step |
| MARY | // Together |
| MARY | // Step step step |
| MARY | Eyes forward, Maitland, or you'll trip |
| MAITLAND | Sadly, I am in no more control of my eyes than I am of my heart, Your Majesty |
| JAMES | Your Privy Council have arrived, we should make a start |
| MARY | // Step |
| MARY | // Together |
| MARY | Can't it wait? |
| MARY | // Step |
| MARY | Isn't this more entertaining? |
| MARY | // Together |

| | |
|---|---|
| JAMES | It would please me if you could remember their names |
| MARY | // Step |
| MARY | Bring them in now then, one after another |
| MARY | // Step |
| MARY | Let's see how they master the delicate nature of our procession |
| MARY | No weapons |
| MARY | No swearing either, I want everyone to be kind |
| MARY | // Step |
| MAITLAND | James Hamilton, Duke of Chatellerault |
| MARY | Ditherer |
| MARY | Protestant |
| DUKE | Your servant, cousin |
| MARY | // Back, together |
| MARY | // Back back back |
| JAMES | James Douglas, Fourth Earl of Morton |
| MARY | Inconstant |
| MARY | Lecherous |
| MARY | Protestant |
| MARY | // Turn together |
| JAMES | Patrick, third Lord Ruthven |
| MARY | Fervent Protestant |
| MAITLAND | Archibald, Earl of Argyll |
| MARY | Protestant |
| MARY | // Turn together |
| JAMES | George Gordon, fourth Earl of Huntly |
| MARY | Once a Catholic |
| MARY | // Turn |

| | |
|---|---|
| MARY | And then a Protestant |
| MARY | // Turn |
| MARY | Then Catholic once again |
| MARY | // Turn |
| HUNTLY | It is my honour to welcome home at last our true Stewart Queen |
| MARY | Cousin, I'm so very pleased you could get away from Aberdeen |
| MARY | // Step together |
| JAMES | Hepburn, fourth Earl of Bothwell |
| MARY | A treasure to my mother |
| MAITLAND | Envious of your brother |
| JAMES | Catholic by name, romantic by nature |
| MARY | // Step together |
| JAMES | Earls of Montrose, Atholl, and Erroll |
| MARY | Roman Catholics |
| MARY | // Step |
| MAITLAND | And the Bishop |
| | All related by marriage |
| JAMES | To me |
| MARY | I see |
| MAITLAND | Erskine |
| | Mar |
| JAMES | Marishcal |
| JAMES | Glencairn |
| MARY | Protestant again |
| JAMES | All related, sooner or later, to me |
| MARY | // Turn together |

| JAMES | The treasurer |
| MAITLAND | And the clerk |
| MARY | Protestant both |
| MARY | // Turn together |
| MARY | I count twice as many Protestants as Roman Catholics on my Privy Council, brother |
| JAMES | Godly men who will be guided by me |
| MARY | // Turn turn turn |
| MAITLAND | You see how we will manage our new Scottish government |
| MARY | // Step together |
| MONTROSE | If I might have a word in your ear, my dear Queen |
| MARY | Of course, Montrose |
| MONTROSE | About the mass on Sunday |
| MARY | // Step together |
| MONTROSE | I would attend |
| MARY | You will be on my arm, dear man, there is nothing I would like more |
| MONTROSE | You're charming but |
| MARY | ? |
| MONTROSE | I hesitate to say |
| MARY | You can say anything to me, sir, you have my ear and my favour |
| MONTROSE | I fear Mr Knockes intends you harm on Sunday |
| MARY | // Step |
| MARY | // Step |
| MARY | // Step |

.

KNOX            When I was first called to preach in this city,
                I gave grateful thanks to the Lord

BRETHREN        // It is right to give thanks and praise

KNOX            Because I found here a welcoming
                congregation of penitent brethren, ready to
                embrace the Word of the Lord, as spoken by
                his son Jesus, who knew that the only way to
                save our souls was to spread that Word here
                on earth
                John Seventeen, I have given them the Word,
                Sanctify them through thy truth
                Our heavenly father sent his only son,
                knowing that he would be mocked, and hated,
                would be hung by his hammered hands to a
                crucifix, would be stabbed with a spear and
                would suffer pain with every breath
                But God so loved His son and His son so
                loved mankind that he gave his very soul
                that we might be saved, that we might be
                one with him
                And what does He ask in return? What does
                He ask in return? Does He ask us to sacrifice
                our sons?

                // No

BRETHREN        // No

KNOX            Does He ask us to stand by as our sons are
                battered and bruised or tortured, our sons,
                whom we love more than ourselves, does He
                ask this of us?
                // No

BRETHREN        // No

KNOX            No
                Does He ask us to forsake all that we love to
                follow Him?
                // No

BRETHREN        // No

KNOX            No
                No
                He asks one thing one thing alone, one thing,
                that we abide in Him and His Word
                Jesus said, now ye are clean through the Word
                which I have spoken unto you
                Now you are clean
                We were clean
                This city was clean, we had already cleansed
                it, and yet not one mile away from this very
                place, the words of the Church of the
                Antichrist are once again being chanted, once
                again that idol of the mass we thought
                banished for ever has wormed its way over
                water and across cursed Catholic lands to
                emerge in its cankerous form within the very
                presence of our Crown, within the breast of
                our very Queen

BRETHREN        // Save our souls

KNOX            The Lord will save us, we have nothing more
                to do but show Him that we will not permit
                this betrayal, that we will not allow this
                desecration of our land, there are those of our
                flock who are already thundering towards that
                very abomination as I stand before you now

BRETHREN        // Howwwwwwwwwwwwl

KNOX            Her idolatry will deliver us to the Devil

# THUNDER

MARY            // Uhhhh

MARY            The first meeting then, as urged by my brother
                and my secretary

MARY            // Huhhh

MARY            The one where he compares us to the mad
                King Nero

| | |
|---|---|
| MARY | John Knockes |
| KNOX | Madam |
| MARY | // Majessssssssty |
| MARY | How dare you drive your unruly mob to my private chapel? |
| KNOX | I did no such (thing) |
| MARY | Where they assaulted my servant and terrified my priest |
| KNOX | who was / (chanting) |
| MARY | // Ssss |
| MARY | If it hadn't been for my brothers guarding the doors, Heaven only knows what mayhem might have transpired |
| MARY | // Ssss |
| MARY | You will raise my people up against me as you did against my mother |
| MARY | // Ssss |
| MARY | Aaaand if that were not enough, you question my authority to rule |
| KNOX | I |
| MARY | You wrote a book, I have it here, *First Blast of the Trumpet Against the Monstrous Regiment of Women*, I am almost out of breath just reading the title |
| KNOX | |
| MARY | A book, I might add, that has cost you your reputation among the most learned in Europe |
| KNOX | |
| MARY | Not least your royal friends in England, sir, I hear the Queen forbids mention of your name in her presence |
| KNOX | It was never |

| MARY | Now, now you threaten my people, my people, with plague, pestilence and fire if they do not support you and your Kirk, and you prophesy these disasters using the Devil only knows what kind of black arts |
| MARY | // Sssss |
| KNOX | … |
| MARY | … |
| KNOX | … |
| MARY | Sir |
| KNOX | You accuse me of so many things, Madam, I hardly know where to begin |
| MARY | I am sure / (you will find the words) |
| KNOX | I listened patiently to Your Majesty, I hope you might offer me the same courtesy |
| MARY | // Uhh |
| KNOX | As to raising your subjects against you, you mistake my mission, Madam, I am instructed by God in His Mercy to teach true knowledge and right worship to men so that they might know and obey their rightful god-fearing ruler |
| MARY | Are you saying I am not their rightful ruler, sir? |
| KNOX | Your Grace cannot see beyond that book |
| MARY | Because you say that I have no authority, by what right? |
| KNOX | The same right that any learned man throughout history has who is able to express his thoughts freely even when those thoughts are unpopular |
| MARY | I have never silenced a scholar |
| KNOX | I made my judgement on women in power in good faith and offered it to the world, but it seems that I am out of step on that matter, |

|  | therefore as long as that is the case I will keep my opinion to myself and be as happy to live under Your Grace as Paul was to live under Nero |
|---|---|
| MARY | // Uhhh |
| MARY | I know who Nero was, sir, and his evil |
| KNOX | I see no good reason why you should take the book personally, as I have said endlessly it was never written with you in mind but against that Jezebel of England, Mary Tudor |
| MARY | You prevaricate, I read your book, sir, and you speak of women in general, women in general are not fit to rule, you say |
| KNOX | As is written in the scriptures, Madam, and from time immemorial |
| MARY | As evidenced by you |
| KNOX | A wiser woman might decide not to bother her head about something that has not yet caused her any trouble, and the plain truth is, Madam, if it had been my intention to cause you harm I might have done it before now and not waited until you came back to Scotland |
| MARY | // Tick |
| MARY | I begin to flail |
| MARY | // Tock |
| MARY | I begin to fail |
| MARY | // Majesty |
| MARY | And yet but yet and yet you have taught my people my people my I you have taught my people another religion than that of their Queen when it is God Himself God who anoints God who commands commands them to obey their rulers |

KNOX        When rulers disobey God, when wicked
            rulers dare disobey God by worshipping
            falsely, Your Majesty, the people are not
            bound to follow

MARY        …but not to raise their swords against them
            surely

KNOX        Unless God grants them the power

MARY        God might grant them the power to slay His
            own anointed ruler?

MARY        // Tick

MARY        And in the failing there is flight, from above
            I see my brother leaning against the heavy
            wooden door picking his nails as if he has no
            care, or care for me at any rate, my secretary of
            state is scribbling this thought or the other in
            advance of some new manipulation and this
            man, this terrible man, this fire-brandishing,
            punishing, wizened man with his sunken eyes
            and zealous words who knows nothing of me,
            nothing, who looks past or through and he
            insults me, he insults me with every line, every
            train of logic designed to defeat me, he would
            stand by, this self-described godly creature, and
            see me hung, drawn and quartered, and raise
            not a finger, I linger over the detail on the
            ceiling where once my mother had painted
            Mary and Francis, from a time when we knew
            what glory was and how to live it, how to bring
            it to our people

KNOX        Madam?

MARY        When Glory was a vision of Heaven on earth,
            a spectacle, a joyous lifting of the heart and
            mind in splendour, this man below will suck
            the life and colour and joy from all of us, will
            punish us for laughter, bend us to him, he will
            never be subject to me

| | |
|---|---|
| JAMES | Sister? |
| MARY | // Majesty |
| MARY | So and so and so |
| MARY | // Marie |
| MARY | And so it seems that my subjects will obey you and not me, they will do as they please and not what I command, and I will be the subject not the Queen |
| KNOX | Only God commands, Madam, and there is no shame in subjecting yourself to Him and his true Church |
| MARY | My Church, sir, the ancient Church of Rome, I think is true |
| KNOX | Your thinking will not make it so, Rome is a whore |
| MARY | // Uhhh |
| KNOX | and corrupts God's true word |
| MARY | My conscience is not corrupt |
| KNOX | Conscience requires right knowledge, Madam, and you have none |
| MARY | I am undone, the floor below me has become insubstantial and I must fix my eyes on a small black bar on the window or I will fall, I will not give this man the satisfaction of seeing my body below him |
| MARY | Go go go |
| KNOX | I pray God that Your Majesty's heart is purged from the venom of idolatry |
| MARY | Go go |
| KNOX | That ye may be blessed |
| MARY | // Go |

| | |
|---|---|
| MARY | Go I say<br>I am already gone |
| | . |
| KNOX | // She is |
| MARY | // He is |
| KNOX | Proud |
| MARY | Cruel |
| KNOX | Crafty |
| MARY | No conversation, only lectures |
| KNOX | No proper education |
| MARY | He makes my blood run cold as he brutally insults me so that I can barely hold myself upright, the breath tightens in my chest and I cannot wait for him to be gone |
| KNOX | Her heart will be forever closed to God |
| MARY | // In truth |
| KNOX | // In truth |
| MARY | I never want to see him again |
| KNOX | I am done with her |
| MARY | And he is done with me |
| MARY | Some days I think I would be better gone |
| MARY | // Uhhh |
| MARY | Oh wheesht, I mean, I need some time in the country, some time on a horse over fields and harrows, this city's narrowness stifles my bones, makes me crampt and crabbit |
| MARY | // Who's with me? |
| | . |
| KNOX | Dear God, our Heavenly Lord whose path through straight and narrow I have followed from the first it was shown to me, whose |

mystery and plan for mankind I have never
doubted even though You have tried me,
Lord, You were there, I know You were there
when I found my beloved wife, in every look,
in every word, in every daily prayer, your
presence touched us both, I had never before
known such happiness and I did not squander
it, I knew it to be a precious gift but why so
short-lived, Lord? and why did she suffer?
She suffered so, no crisis of faith or love but a
body wracked and tormented by mortal agony
and I have asked you, begged you, to show
me why, when you could have taken me who
is older who is riven with sin, why oh why
did you take my innocent Marjorie and leave
me bereft, my bride, my bedfellow who loved
me, I am downcast

And obdurate as I must appear to you, my
lords, which could not be further from the
truth, for I have known joy but my fragile
heart breaks to see this country slide back into
idolatry, breaks to watch evil slip in through
the cracks of wavering faith

And I am cast down by the weight of every
day having to remind you that only through
purity can we be truly saved

I have given this matter considerable reflection
and have concluded that the day is nigh when
we must make a stand against our sovereign

// Who's with me?

| | |
|---|---|
| LORD | You will chase her away |
| LORD | She is only just arrived |
| LORD | A civilised country is nothing without a court |
| LORD | Our nobility has scare survived interminable wars |
| LORD | We want some stability |

| | |
|---|---|
| LORD | Some sort of opportunities for our daughters and sons |
| LORD | Would you plunge us back into uncertainty, sir? |
| KNOX | The Kirk session would forbid her the mass |
| LORD | But what if she keeps it private? |
| LORD | And none of us go |
| LORD | Nor any other good soul |
| LORD | She will be alone in her chapel with a terrified mumbling priest |
| LORD | Anxious to be done |
| LORD | To be gone |
| KNOX | Will you condemn this poor realm once again to the plague and vengeance which will inevitably follow? |
| LORD | No need to take it to extremes, John |
| LORD | // What's the harm? |
| KNOX | All those in favour of banning her private mass, say Aye? |
| LORD | // I say no |
| LORD | // No |
| LORD | // No |
| LORD | // No |
| LORD | // No |
| LORD | // No |
| KNOX | And so do the votes of the lords prevail against the Kirk's ministers |
| | . |
| MARY | Whispers are the very fabric of the palace |
| MARY | Hidden panels |

| | |
|---|---|
| MARY | Trapdoors |
| MARY | Corridors where heads spring apart as soon as we enter |
| MARY | Messengers whose letters may have already been waylaid and resealed |
| MARY | Whose contents offer nothing more than best regards |
| MARY | But whose secrets are revealed in hurried tones as if the carrier must unburden himself or perish |
| MARY | Invitations to hunt |
| MARY | Hawk |
| MARY | Golf |
| MARY | Crossbow and arrow |
| MARY | Make war |
| MARY | Marry this one or the other |
| MARY | Do as her brother tells her |
| MARY | And his secretary, Maitland |
| MAITLAND | Your only stability is to be found through Elizabeth or a husband |
| MARY | He says, as if I am a child |
| MAITLAND | Have her name you successor and no one will shake your tenure |
| | Gain her approval of a husband, we should write to Her Majesty |
| | A delicate expression of your heart's desire that she should know you better, were she only to meet you face to face |
| MARY | Am I right to be suspicious? |
| | I believe you are a spy, William Maitland |
| | You copy everything I say and send it to her secretary as you did with my mother |

| | |
|---|---|
| MARY | Every meeting |
| MARY | Every ambassador |
| MARY | Every plan for the future |
| MARY | Monitor of every phrase every gesture |
| MARY | Why should I keep you at my side? |
| MARY | Your solemn oath that you will never again betray me |
| MARY | // By Almighty God |
| MAITLAND | You have my word |
| MARY | Or I will know it and that will be an end to your time in Scotland |
| MAITLAND | A union between Your Majesty and Elizabeth will bring the family of the United Kingdom into being, a dream we all share |
| MARY | I will call her sister |
| MARY | // Ssss |
| MARY | Ask for her sisterly advice |
| MARY | On matters of the heart |
| MARY | We might begin with a few lines of verse |
| MARY | We hear she writes in Latin, Italian and French |
| MARY | Like ourselves |
| MARY | And we shall talk about how dull and boring it is to be lectured by old men |
| MARY | Gossiped about by jealous women |
| MARY | Complimented by impostors |
| MARY | Married on to halfwits and children |
| MARY | And how we shall laugh |
| MARY | We might talk of husbands |
| MARY | Children |
| MARY | The threat of rebellion |

| | |
|---|---|
| MARY | To our property |
| MARY | And person |
| MARY | No one knows better than we two the perils of a regnant queen |
| MARY | // Chop |
| MAITLAND | Apart from her mother |
| MARY | Indeed |
| MAITLAND | Offer her your agreement before you even meet, as if it were the simplest thing to achieve |
| MARY | There is nothing easier, I am eager to recognise her as Queen of England |
| MAITLAND | Unconditionally |
| MARY | Until such times as she departs this life, you know she barely survived the pox |
| MARY | // Uhhh |
| MARY | And then I would take her place at the head of our United Kingdoms |
| MAITLAND | Let me find a better way of phrasing your proposition |
| MARY | Of course |
| MARY | Ahem |
| MARY | Pssss |
| MARY | Aye |
| MARY | Husband |
| MARY | Bye the bye |
| MAITLAND | Majesty? |
| MARY | While you're in London, you will be sure to call in to the Spanish Embassy to hear news of Don Carlos and our marriage proposal |
| MAITLAND | With the utmost delicacy |

MARY        We would bring this country to its rightful
            position in Europe

            .

KNOX        Your Esteemed Majesty,

MARY        My good Sister Queen

KNOX        // It cannot have escaped Your Majesty's
            attention that

MARY        // It cannot have escaped Your Majesty's
            attention that

MARY        Nothing would give me greater joy than that
            we two might meet

KNOX        The Protestant Kingdoms of Scotland and
            England have been placed in jeopardy with
            the arrival of the Papist Queen from France

MARY        In token of my great esteem I have sent you
            my most prized ring

KNOX        I spoke with her in recent days and find her to
            be two-faced and wily

MARY        A gift from my beloved mother

KNOX        I have every reason to believe it is her firm
            intention to follow the lead provided by her
            murderous uncles and your sister, that other
            Marie, to wage a bloody war against our
            godly Reformation

KNOX        // I believe further
MARY        // I believe further

MARY        That we should no sooner meet than we
            should find ourselves to be the best of friends

KNOX        She cannot be trusted with Your Majesty's
            person

MARY        It would give me the sweetest pleasure to
            welcome you here in Scotland, or travel into
            your kingdom, should that be your desire

| | |
|---|---|
| KNOX | Her insatiable greed and envy will not stop within the boundaries of this kingdom but will advance, as soon as ever she can, into your own |
| MARY | // There is nothing in this world that would give me greater happiness than to finally call you dear sister, face to face |
| KNOX | There is nothing I regret more than not taking stronger action, for that vile idol of the mass corrupts our very air like blackest plague, and we are harder pressed to cleanse our kingdom once again, without your aid I am afraid we will be lost to Satan |
| MARY | // Pray let me hear from you soon |
| KNOX | // Pray let me hear from you soon |
| KNOX | Pray God it is not already too late |
| MARY | Your Sister Queen |
| KNOX | With troubled heart |
| MARY | Marie |
| | . |
| MARY | Now, Marys, which fine husbands do you propose? |
| MARY | In order? |
| MARY | Don Carlos should be top of the list |
| MARY | On one hand, Don Carlos is the Catholic prince of Spain |
| MARY | Wealthy |
| MARY | Powerful |
| MARY | Seventeen |
| MARY | Armies in his train |
| MARY | On the other |
| MARY | Inbred |

| MARY | Delicate |
| MARY | Deformed |
| MARY | Unpredictable |
| MARY | Seventeen though |
| MARY | // Hmm |
| MARY | Or |
| MARY | Charles the Ninth |
| MARY | My dead husband's brother |
| MARY | But his mother |
| MARY | My dead husband's mother |
| MARY | Is unwilling |
| MARY | Unforgiving |
| MARY | There was no offence given on my part |
| MARY | But by your uncles, you may recall |
| MARY | The whole Guise family are on her bad side |
| MARY | Besides |
| MARY | Charles the Ninth is only ten years old |
| MARY | There have been younger matches |
| MARY | I was older than his brother |
| MARY | By a year |
| MARY | Neither here nor there |
| MARY | But your mother-in-law's daughter, your dead husband's sister, is married to Don Carlos's father |
| MARY | Which would make your cousin your mother |
| MARY | In-law |
| MARY | // Ooo |
| MARY | Awkward |

| | |
|---|---|
| MARY | And the people don't want a Catholic |
| MARY | You mean the Reformers |
| MARY | They say it wouldn't be politic |
| MARY | Another? |
| MARY | Archduke Charles of Austria |
| MARY | Hapsburg |
| MARY | Son of an emperor |
| MARY | Twenty |
| MARY | One year older |
| MARY | Also a suitor to Good Queen Bess |
| MARY | Suitable nonetheless |
| MARY | But his brother |
| MARY | King Maximilian |
| MARY | Tolerant, like you |
| MARY | Is jealous |
| MARY | And has forbidden it so far |
| MARY | // Aww |
| MARY | Are there any others? |
| MARY | How do you like Sweden? |
| MARY | Cold |
| MARY | Northern |
| MARY | Surrounded by islands |
| MARY | Unpronounceable vowels |
| MARY | Alfonso then, Duke of Ferrara |
| MARY | Twenty-nine |
| MARY | His wife was a Medici |
| MARY | Like your husband's mother |
| MARY | // Another |

| | |
|---|---|
| MARY | Prince of Condé, cousin to your mother |
| MARY | Protestant Reformer |
| MARY | The people would love it |
| MARY | Cousin to my mother? |
| MARY | // Eeeooo |
| MARY | No rustic Scotsmen to tempt me? |
| MARY | John Gordon, of Huntly |
| MARY | Uncultured |
| MARY | Or the Earl of Arran |
| MARY | Unhinged I hear |
| MARY | Or or |
| MARY | The Earl of Leicester |
| MARY | Dudley? |
| MARY | A commoner |
| MARY | Lover to Queen Elizabeth? |
| MARY | Are there no others? |
| MARY | It is early in your reign |
| MARY | Are we so undesirable? |
| MARY | // Never |
| MARY | It's a barren time, it seems, for suitable princes |
| MARY | For all of us |
| MARY | You might wait a little longer |
| MARY | I'm afraid that, unless I become a wife and mother a son, my future is over, I sit with little power between Catholic Spain and Protestant England and am hourly waiting to be informed that my country is no longer my own but belongs to a Reformer, say another then |
| MARY | // Say another |
| MARY | // Say another |

MARY            Then I will have Don Carlos, deformed or not

                .

MARY            // Sidestep sidestep[3]

MARY            // Back step sidestep

MARY            // Skip turn skip turn

MARY            // Wag wag wag

MARY            Now this is a pretty sight, our Holyrood
                Château restored

MARY            Gold and silverware

MARY            Dazzling lights

MARY            Tapestries, rugs, cushions and silks

MARY            White-linen tablecloths

MARY            Musicians to amuse, on their trumpets, oboes,
                violas and lutes

MARY            To say nothing of the lords and ladies of our
                court

MARY            Fashionably dressed

MARY            At last

MARY            Dancing as if they were Spanish or Italian

MARY            Everything exquisitely made

MARY            Everything a banquet requires

MARY            Including a masquerade

MARY            Featuring an encounter between a Virgin
                Queen and a Scottish ambassador

MARY            As they contemplate a portrait of Her
                Majesty, Queen of Scots

MARY            I pray they will not find it wanting

                .

---

3. Dançe: Branle des lavandières

BESS              Tell me, sir, is she as tall as they say?

AMBASSADOR She is tall enough

BESS              Taller than I?

AMBASSADOR By the merest inch or so

BESS              And this portrait, does it do her justice?

AMBASSADOR As much as your own Majesty's

BESS              Her face is very pale in the painting, has she
                  covered up marks or scars? She never had the
                  pox, I trust?

AMBASSADOR She is naturally pale, Your Majesty's face
                  shows every sign of recovery

BESS              Is she fat? I saw a painting of Anne of Cleves
                  where she looked like a splinter of oak and
                  when she turned up we thought she was
                  padded as a joke

AMBASSADOR She takes regular exercise, Ma'am, to keep
                  herself strong

BESS              Does she suffer from weakness then?

AMBASSADOR An occasional turn

BESS              Hmmm

AMBASSADOR But she is well now

BESS              I hear she dances, is she clumsy on the turn?
                  Tall people are often cursed with gangling
                  limbs, does she falter at the quickness?

AMBASSADOR  She dances no better nor worse than any
                  educated in the steps

BESS              Does she play chess? I play, would she be
                  a match for me?

AMBASSADOR I couldn't perfectly say, however I do know
                  that nothing would give her greater happiness
                  than to be sat at the table opposite you
                  engaged in that very game

| | |
|---|---|
| BESS | I know, but I can't persuade my weasel of a secretary who's taken it into his head that she'd rather have my crown instead of her own |
| AMBASSADOR | I assure Your Majesty, your Sister Queen is perfectly happy where she is and would cut off her right hand before causing you a moment's harm |
| BESS | I tend to agree and I think before long I may go visit my little Scottish sister |
| MARY | Nothing would bring me greater happiness |
| MARY | // Elizabeth |
| MARY | And in the meantime let's show them how we dance, and with what quickness |
| MARY | // Sidestep sidestep |
| MARY | // Back step sidestep |
| MARY | // Skip turn skip turn |
| MARY | // Wag wag wag |
| | . |
| KNOX | She did what? |
| SPY | Danced |
| KNOX | Upon receiving the news of the murderous deaths in France, you say? |
| SPY | Danced harder and louder, her lords leapt, the court has never been merrier |
| KNOX | As her uncles butcher the godly brethren |
| SPY | Energetic dancing with clapping, skipping, birling and the like |
| KNOX | Dancing like harlots, no doubt, more suited to the brothel than a god-fearing court |
| SPY | Ladies being lifted clear off the floor |

| | |
|---|---|
| MARY | // fffffff |
| KNOX | Flighty fillocks who shame their ancestry |
| SPY | Till three maybe four in the morning, and there was wine |
| | . |
| MARY | He said what?!!! |
| LORD | He cried it from the pulpit this very Sunday |
| LORD | He said you should be crushed |
| LORD | With iron |
| LORD | Broken in pieces like a potter's urn |
| LORD | That you are a raging heathen |
| MARY | // Knockes |
| MARY | A second meeting then |
| MARY | The one where he gave us to know we were completely alone |
| MARY | This time we vow to be as stubbornly present as he |
| | . |
| KNOX | And you will have also heard from your courtiers that I spoke at length on the subject of the dignity and honour of kings? |
| MARY | My lords? |
| LORD | // He did |
| LORD | // He did but |
| KNOX | And of a biblical kingdom where criminals might prosper under a prince who cares more for fiddling and dancing than reading or hearing God's own Word |
| MARY | And whose kingdom might that be, sir? |
| KNOX | Why, Nero's, for one |

| | |
|---|---|
| MARY | Lords? |
| LORD | // Yes he did |
| LORD | // He did but |
| KNOX | Fiddling and dancing while God's children are banished and murdered |
| MARY | It was reported to me somewhat differently |
| KNOX | Altered, no doubt, for your favour |
| MARY | I was informed that you criticised your Queen, that you spoke of me without respect, worse, you invited my subjects to condemn me and to hate me |
| KNOX | I am not surprised to hear it |
| MARY | Crushed with iron, broken like a potter's urn |
| KNOX | They clearly did not recognise the second psalm |
| MARY | And that you were particularly damning about the dancing at court |
| KNOX | I had something to say of dancing, I will admit |
| LORD | // You see |
| MARY | The selfsame courtly dancing that is admired in civilised countries, that by its very nature encourages fine behaviour and manners? |
| KNOX | I will not pretend to like it, I find it an abomination, it is the vanity of the unfaithful |
| LORD | // He said that |
| KNOX | But try as I might I can find no direct condemnation of it in the Lord's gospels and so I must tolerate it |
| LORD | // And that |
| MARY | I do not ask for your permission, sir, the Kirk is yours the Court is mine |

| | |
|---|---|
| KNOX | But but I will speak out against it when those dancing demean themselves by their actions |
| MARY | Sir, by your own admission you know nothing of the practice, your cautionary words are superfluous |
| KNOX | Or when it is used in celebration of the tragedies that befall God's chosen flock, as was practised by the Philistines |
| MARY | Which everyone here will deny, we celebrated a marriage |
| KNOX | You bring me to the nub of things, Madam, it is clear to me that you have surrounded yourself with claw-backs and flea-borne parasites who will whisper whatever you like in your ears and divorce themselves from the plain truth in order to win your favour, brightly clothed insects whose words are patently not to be trusted and who will now attest in front of you that what they had previously reported was false |
| MARY | My lords? |
| LORD | // He said what he said |
| LORD | // He did |
| LORD | // But not in that manner |
| KNOX | And who will now scrabble like crabs in a barrel, caught between Your Grace and the plain truth, I wonder not that you have been so misguided |
| MARY | You are harsh, sir, and perhaps we have both been somewhat misled, might I ask that in the future, if you hear gossip about my person, you come to me with it before you announce it in the Kirk session |
| KNOX | You would have me run to you every time I hear something ill, some new piece of tittle-tattle? You mistake my calling |

| | |
|---|---|
| MARY | I ask only for the opportunity to acknowledge or deny the accusations before hearing them aired publicly |
| KNOX | I am instructed by God to rebuke the sins and vices of all, I have no time to tell every man his offence |
| MARY | I am not every man, sir |
| KNOX | Let me recommend you to my sermons, Madam, three times a week and Sundays, should you wish to further our acquaintance, otherwise you will find me at my book |
| | . |
| MARY | // Raaaaaaaaaaar |
| MARY | There is not one ounce of softness in the man |
| MARY | He sniggered as he left |
| MARY | Why should I be afraid of a pretty face? |
| MARY | // He said |
| MARY | When I have stood up to angrier men and not faltered |
| MARY | May he not come back again |
| MARY | I am at my wit's end to know how to appease him, he will not be charmed |
| MAITLAND | But he does you no real harm yet your popularity grows with every visit you make to north and south, the people in the cities line up to catch the merest sight of you |
| MARY | I feel welcomed by them, it's true, I noticed more of them on the streets as we rode through Perth and Fife |
| MARY | Diana, they call you |
| MARY | Sweet face |
| MARY | Voice of a goddess |

MARY            Angel in a saddle

MARY            There is no grey with Mr Knockes, he sees
                everything as either black or white

MAITLAND        A period of quiet might serve you well, no
                show of the mass, no flagrant encouragement
                of your favourites, a more intimate company
                for music and dance

MARY            It feels like a punishment when he is the one
                who shows me no tolerance and I am always
                having to temper myself

MAITLAND        You have the nature for it, Majesty, it has
                already been remarked here and abroad,
                Queen Elizabeth is rumoured to be jealous of
                your delicate manners

MARY            I write her almost daily, I send jewellery and
                portraits, verses and the dearest words I can
                conjure, she is not averse to a meeting, I am
                sure of it

MAITLAND        If only out of curiosity

MARY            She last wrote that she favoured York for
                our meeting and we are already preparing
                a banquet and masquerades, but for Knockes
                I might be almost happy

                    .

BRETHREN        A mass was said in Maybole

BRETHREN        And one in Inverness

BRETHREN        Strathbogle

BRETHREN        Aberdeen

BRETHREN        Countless places in the west and further afield

KNOX            Look how brave men grow under tolerance

BRETHREN        In the open

BRETHREN        In neglected chapels

BRETHREN    In each other's houses

BRETHREN    To crowds

KNOX    And yet I hear our lords plead for men to have liberty to practise what they will, that a civilised country must encourage debate, as if Paul had never written that the scriptures are there for our instruction, but we are promised the wrath of God if we bend over backwards towards Satan, who stands by greedily licking his lips as the souls of good men are trampled in the race toward worldly riches, liberty to practice, mark me well, is nothing more nor less than extending an invitation to the Devil

BRETHREN    // Saints preserve us

KNOX    Those priests have broken God's solemn law, they are criminal

BRETHREN    Arrest them

BRETHREN    Charge them

BRETHREN    Imprison them

BRETHREN    Hang them

KNOX    One mass, I said, that first Queen's mass was more fearful to me than a thousand strong army waging war against us and so it has been proven, the Lord will have His vengeance

.

MARY    Might we be lenient, Master Knockes? These men are priests, as you once were, I might add

KNOX    The Devil comes cloaked in many forms, Madam, it is testimony to my youth and the lack of the Evangel in Scotland that I was so hoodwinked

MARY    But not evil

KNOX    It's a simple matter of the law, and the law which you agreed to uphold before you

|  | returned states that there will be no public mass without sanctions |
|---|---|
| MARY | These men in Ayr who have taken the priests have no right to dispense justice in my name |
| KNOX | They do no more than uphold Your Majesty's governance, it will be widely regarded as shameful if you withhold your support |
| MARY | I wonder now at imagining I might |
| KNOX | You might imagine any number of things but your duty, Madam, is to the righteous |
| MARY | Indeed |
| KNOX | And they will not be placated, they will see justice |
| MARY | Master Knockes |
| KNOX | With or without your permission |
| MARY | There is no need to threaten me with rebellion, I am persuaded |
| KNOX | … |
| MARY | I will accept your counsel on this occasion |
| KNOX | God be praised that your mind is not yet hardened (to true discipline) |
| MARY | But the dispensing of the punishment will lie with me |
| KNOX | Your Majesty |
| MARY | But wait |
| KNOX | I can offer you no more on the subject |
| MARY | I would like to speak a little longer with you, sir |
| KNOX | I am wanted in Ayr |
| MARY | A moment only |

| | |
|---|---|
| KNOX | … |
| MARY | You will think me foolish |
| KNOX | … |
| MARY | But I wonder if I might ask |
| KNOX | … |
| MARY | Do you believe me to be bad? |
| KNOX | // I |
| MARY | // I mean, as I stand here in front of you, tell me in all honesty, is what you see a person with a bad heart, with vile intent? |
| KNOX | In which / sense? |
| MARY | / without deliberation, without rummaging through your vast biblical reference for corroboration, just |
| KNOX | There is no better history of experience than that good book |
| MARY | Look, now I offer these few moments wherein you and I might speak with honesty |
| KNOX | My speech is always // so |
| MARY | // So that we might avert a greater tragedy and the moment is almost past, the moment within which we might change everything, you will fritter away with verbosity |
| KNOX | You have a foreshortened view of the future and I am not sure… |
| MARY | With good cause, sir, if it were up to you I might be gone tomorrow |
| KNOX | …that any good will prosper if we are to continue |
| MARY | Let me begin again, will you wait? |
| KNOX | I am yours to command |

| | |
|---|---|
| MARY | I doubt it… not… what I meant was not to question but to state that when I look at you, sir, face to face across this reachable space, I do not see a bad man |
| KNOX | It could not be otherwise |
| MARY | I do not see a bad man but I see a man who wishes me harm, I see a man who will every Sunday and three times a week harangue a congregation into hating my very being, so I ask you once again, when you look at me here, eye to eye, do you see a bad person? |
| KNOX | I |
| MARY | A bad woman |
| KNOX | I |
| MARY | Because every day of my god-given life since before the age of five, when I last lived in this country, my waking thought, my last before I sleep is do well, think well, give thanks to God every day, it is my daily practice, my daily intent |
| KNOX | If intent were all, there would be no road to damnation |
| MARY | Will you waste it then, this precious time with none but you and I to hear the truth between us? |
| KNOX | You will not want to hear what I see |
| MARY | It has never stopped you from expressing it before // now |
| KNOX | // Now I see a child, an undereducated girl, catapulted into a station beyond her ability to govern, a girl who would rather spend time with flattering poets and violas and dance than embrace the ineluctable future of this nation |
| MARY | Don't forget my passion for horses in your condemnation |

| | |
|---|---|
| KNOX | A girl who at the slightest opportunity will reduce everything to whimsy |
| MARY | You are harsh, sir, I've come to expect no less, but even so I will proceed because it is in my nature to extract what little good I can, be it well-nigh invisible |
| KNOX | I do not speak for your pleasure |
| MARY | Rather to undermine me, I'm sure, but in all of that, my youth, my inexperience, my joyousness, yet you fail to address my question, Do you think I am a bad person? |
| KNOX | I fail to see what is to be had from a continuance |
| MARY | It is this alone, that if, for once, in private session, we might bare each other's fears and ambitions, then we might the better live divided in harmony |
| KNOX | That such a notion even crosses your mind is testament to an inability to think |
| MARY | So I am bad then, in your view? |
| KNOX | There can be no two ways about how to live the true life, the division you speak of would mean to walk alongside Satan |
| MARY | Come now, you're avoiding the issue almost as if you are afraid to say the words |
| KNOX | I am afraid of no man, living or dead |
| MARY | Perhaps yourself then |
| KNOX | My fears for myself I confess to my God |
| MARY | And no other? |
| KNOX | You are confusing the girlish tattle that passes for conversation at court, Madam, with an examination of thought |

MARY      Is it to be so, then, I offer you honesty at some
          cost and you give nought of yourself?

KNOX      Not so

MARY      You must think me very bad // indeed

KNOX      // Indeed I do… not

MARY      You do not?

KNOX      No again

MARY      When you look at me you do not see a bad
          woman?

KNOX      It does not change with repetition

MARY      No you say, three times no, now there's
          something to be had after all from an informal
          meeting and open exchange, we have come to
          some kind of agreement at last, a tentative
          beginning, no more than the smallest of
          platforms on which to perform, but a small
          thing is better than none, I think

KNOX      I fear there is worse

MARY      Of course you will say something now to
          make my heart sink, but I will hold on for
          dear life to that small crumb of a No

KNOX      I can see along with any man that you are not
          bad, you have all the faults I named before,
          and along with those an intuition from the
          Devil knows where to divine my fear of
          myself in my reluctance to speak

MARY      Stop now, please, Mister Knockes, we might
          continue another day, my mother used to say
          to me, know when you have achieved even a
          small victory

KNOX      A victory?

MARY      Shared by us both, not one over the other, sir

| | |
|---|---|
| KNOX | As to that, we might discuss it later |
| MARY | An excellent thought, later was the very time I had in mind |
| KNOX | But now that we are here at a beginning, it would be unnatural of you not to hear my fear aloud |
| MARY | You think me churlish, but truly that intuition you speak of has fired a dreaded clattering in my heart, let's start anew another day, I beg |
| KNOX | I will go then, Madam, but let time show that your offer was to speak but not to listen |
| MARY | And how will it show, sir? |
| KNOX | History will tell it so |
| MARY | History will know nothing of it |
| KNOX | If you say so |
| MARY | I confess I am more afraid of your fear than my own, I feel sure it will rebound on me |
| KNOX | My fear for myself is no more, no less than my vanity, even as I call myself chosen I must counter it with 'as the lowest of men', when I claim to hear and preach God's word I remind myself it is because I surrender my heart and soul to an eternally loving Master who does not speak to me as a special favour, many men before me are alive to His Word, I claim not to be an apostle but merely a pupil |
| MARY | I believe it of you, sir, you are good to say it |
| KNOX | And no sooner do I consider myself good than I am struck dumb by my own self-loving, which turns immediately to loathing |
| MARY | You are harsh even on yourself, I see |
| KNOX | Days can pass when I cannot rise or eat, when the weight of my own worthless life lies so heavily on me that my legs will not stand, |

weeks when, were it not for my colleagues and beloved friends, I would perish, I beg God to bring me to his bosom as soon as he can for I am almost done with the daily struggle

MARY    This is a great comfort to me, I am also felled by sadness on many an occasion, overwhelmed by

KNOX    But when you summon me here to your whispering chamber, when you ask me in your childlike manner if I think you are a bad person because otherwise why would I preach against you in the Kirk three times a week and Sunday, then I thank God for my vanity, for my ability to see how magnified it might become in one so misguided, one who so wilfully mistakes my preaching the sacred text as an insult towards her person

MARY    I

KNOX    Who but a misbegotten child of the Devil's Church would reconstruct the writings of the Bible, the torture and martyrdom of Holy Saints, the repentance of sinners and the judgements of men who were giants, as a reference to her temporal behaviour?

MARY    I

KNOX    Who but an abandoned infant would bawl and mewl in the face of the proper food of the Lord and His son, Jesus Christ? Who but...

MARY    No more

KNOX    ...an ill-prepared, ill-informed, foolish girl would pit her insignificant wit against a trained theologian and imagine to lure him into her confidence with her simpering smile and puckering chin

MARY    Sir

KNOX    I am not taken in by you, Madam

| | |
|---|---|
| MARY | … |
| KNOX | … |
| MARY | I may be all of those things but I am not misbegotten |
| KNOX | I should never have come |
| MARY | I have been as truly loved as one might hope for, as I hope you have too, sir |
| KNOX | You should not have invited me |
| MARY | But how else might we know each other better? |
| KNOX | There is no knowing between us, we are in eternal opposition |
| MARY | I am sorry for it |
| KNOX | As am I, for you will suffer |
| MARY | And will you be glad of it? |
| KNOX | Enough |
| MARY | And what will history say of this, sir? |
| KNOX | History will hear nothing of it |
| | . |
| KNOX | I want to know when they dance, how high, when they sing, which song, who comes in, who goes out, who is loitering in passageways reciting poetic ballads, slipping into adulterous beds, sending and receiving dispatches, having unsuitable dalliances, I want news from France and Spain before the messenger has booked his passage, I want every hint of connivance between Maitland and his alliances, I can be disturbed night and day when the information will serve to unsettle this unholy court |
| | . |
| MARY | // Sssss |

MARY            Stirling is more out of the way

MARY            // Shhhh

MARY            Sheltered from the ever-present guard who
                may or may not be trusted, who may be in my
                brother's

MARY            // Step

MARY            Pay or Knockes's

MARY            // Ssss

MARY            Out of the city in the cradle of my early years
                I am surrounded by more loyal souls old
                enough to remember my father

MARY            // Himmmmmmmmmmmmmmmm

MARY            Whose love of grandeur is remembered in
                every bow and curtsy

MARY            Your Majesty

MARY            A visitor

MARY            From abroad

MARY            // What news

MARY            What word

MARY            Religious war in France

MARY            Your uncles against the Huguenots

MARY            Elizabeth has sent her army to oppose them

MARY            She looks to you for support

MARY            As do my uncles

MARY            Her plan for the banquet and masquerades at
                the meeting in York

MARY            How should we reply?

MARY            I must take a neutral stand, my realm is
                unready to enter into an affray

MARY            What word?

| | |
|---|---|
| MARY | Ambiguity from Spain, your mother-in-law |
| MARY | // As was |
| MARY | Is poisoning the ear of Philip the Second |
| MARY | Putting Don Carlos out of reach as a husband |
| MARY | Our crown will be diminished if I cannot make a match |
| MARY | What news, what news |
| MARY | A visitor in disguise |
| MESSENGER | The Holy Roman Pope is mystified at your lack of progress, the future of our religion in your isles is wholly dependant upon your intercession |
| MARY | There can be no open Catholicism practised in view of the volatility of our situation |
| MARY | Italy will find it harder to support your treasury |
| MARY | It is outwith my control |
| MARY | A messenger from France |
| MARY | A messenger from Italy |
| MARY | A messenger from Spain |
| MARY | I am failing |
| MESSENGER | // We regret |
| MESSENGER | There will be no money |
| MESSENGER | We cannot confirm a marriage yet |
| MESSENGER | No soldiers |
| MESSENGER | Nor jewels from your previous reign |
| MESSENGER | // You are letting us all down |
| MARY | And from London? |
| MESSENGER | Queen Elizabeth is sorry to say that she cannot meet you after all |

MARY            My elaborate fabrication of our sisterhood
                unravels like a delicate lace veil

MESSENGER       Given the circumstances in France and your
                connection to their nobility, she's afraid it
                would be seen as a betrayal and sends her
                sincerest apology

MARY            I fail I fail

                .

KNOX            My lords, without funds the Reformation of this
                once blessed  country will founder, I entreat
                you transfer those Roman Catholic properties
                and their incomes to the Scottish Kirk

LORD            Impossible

LORD            Would you beggar us?

KNOX            At the very least you must insist that she
                confirm the Parliament we constituted with
                our confession of faith

LORD            She is considering

KNOX            In honour of the dangers we faced together on
                battlefields against her mother on these very
                Crags of Edinburgh

LORD            The battles are over

LORD            We've already won

LORD            Why must you harp on about bloodshed and
                lightning

LORD            It was fighting that killed our fathers and their
                fathers before them

KNOX            Had Delilah conjured a fabulous world before
                your very eyes you could not be more blinded
                by glistering promise of titles and favours
                whilst behind your back she reaches into your
                coffers and steals your most valuable prize,
                your hard-fought Reformation, will you for

|  | God's love enshrine it in law that our Queen must never marry a Roman Catholic? |
|---|---|
| LORD | My wife |
| LORD | Brother |
| LORD | Uncle |
| LORD | Father |
| LORD | // Is Catholic |
| LORD | Or was |
| LORD | Her heart is her own |
| LORD | Let her alone for a while |
| KNOX | I am done, the lone voice in a desert of worldly dissent, I can no longer fight, my God, was I chosen only to be forsaken? |
|  | . |
| GOSSIP | whisper |
| GOSSIP | whisper |
| GOSSIP | whisper |
| GOSSIP | whisper |
| SPY | Mister Ambassador |
| GOSSIP | tittle-tattle |
| GOSSIP | tittle-tattle |
| GOSSIP | tittle-tattle |
| SPY | Catholic |
| GOSSIP | disastrous |
| GOSSIP | disastrous |
| GOSSIP | disastrous |
| GOSSIP | disastrous |
| SPY | Hispanic |

| | |
|---|---|
| GOSSIP | alliance |
| GOSSIP | alliance |
| GOSSIP | alliance |
| GOSSIP | alliance |
| SPY | Marriage |
| GOSSIP | Don Carlos Don Carlos Don Carlos Don Carlos |
| GOSSIP | Don Carlos Don Carlos Don Carlos Don Carlos |
| GOSSIP | Don Carlos Don Carlos Don Carlos Don Carlossssss |
| GOSSIP | **SSS SSS SSS SSSSSSSSSSSSSSSSSS** |
| KNOX | SSSSScotland will be consigned to everlasting damnation when its Queen, God rescue her from Satan's grasp, allies her crown with that of Papist Spain, note this day and note it well, my lords and earls, that when you allow Don Carlos, that Infidel, to become King over our weak female sovereign you banish Christ Jesus from this realm and invite God's blackest vengeance |
| MARY | KNOCKES |
| MARY | Again |
| MARY | The time when he reduces us to tears |
| MARY | Bring him to me bring him bring him |
| KNOX | Madam |
| MARY | You |
| KNOX | … |
| MARY | You you you I have put up with you, I have put up with your harsh words, your your insulting (manner) |
| MARY | // Mmmmmmmmmmmm |

| | |
|---|---|
| KNOX | … |
| MARY | The way you speak to me has been intolerable from the very first |
| MARY | // Mmmmmmmmmmmm |
| MARY | If this had been France… |
| MARY | // Mmmmmmmmmmmm |
| MARY | …you would… |
| MARY | // Mmmmmmmmmmmm |
| MARY | …you would have been pilloried, sir, head of the church or no, you you would never have … |
| MARY | // Mmmmmmmmmmmm |
| MARY | …dared to talk of me or to me as you do |
| KNOX | … |
| MARY | // Mmmmmmmmmmmm |
| MARY | And I have been kind to you |
| MARY | // Mmmmmmmmmmmm |
| MARY | While you rant and rebuke me as if I were… |
| MARY | // Mmmmmmmmmmmm |
| MARY | …a child, not the sovereign of your land and |
| KNOX | … |
| MARY | // Mmmmmmmmmmmm |
| MARY | You give nothing, sir, nothing in return, nothing |
| KNOX | … |
| MARY | I am the Queen |
| MARY | // Mmmmmmmmmmmm |
| KNOX | … |

| | |
|---|---|
| MARY | Do you hear me, sir? I am the Queen |
| KNOX | … |
| MARY | And just who in my realm do you think you are? |
| KNOX | … |
| MARY | … |
| KNOX | A citizen born and bred, no more, no less |
| MARY | // Mmmmmmmmmmmm |
| KNOX | Commanded by God to do His bidding |
| MARY | // Mmmmmmmmmmmm |
| KNOX | To speak out when His flock is in danger |
| MARY | What on earth has any of that got to do with my marriage? |
| MARY | // Mmmmmmmmmmmm |
| KNOX | When your marriage threatens God's children with plague and pestilence, my tongue belongs not to me but to the Lord |
| MARY | // Mmmmmmmmmmmm |
| KNOX | No thought of offence informs my judgement where my conscience is concerned |
| MARY | // Mmmmmmmmmmmm |
| KNOX | But there is nothing in my words that deserves this outpouring of tears, this inordinate passion which I struggle to believe comes from any rational consideration but is rooted in thwarted anger |
| MARY | // Mmmmmmmmmmmm |
| MARY | Get him out of my sight |
| KNOX | I pray God may soften Your Majesty's heart |
| MARY | I pray we never speak again, sir |

| | |
|---|---|
| KNOX | Your tears and prayers, Madam, will not silence me |
| MARY | Leave me |
| KNOX | With pleasure, Majesty, for I am done with this court and it is done with me |
| MARY | / Aaaaahhhhhhhhhhhhhhhhhhhhhhhh-hhhhhhhhhhh |
| MARY | Bring him back here |
| MARY | Get him gone |

# SLAM

.

| | |
|---|---|
| MARY | // Uhh |
| MARY | And we have taken to our bed |
| MARY | Insensible |
| MARY | Unwell |
| MARY | Unable to sleep |
| MARY | To speak |
| MARY | Or chew |
| MARY | Brews of every tempting fruit and herb trickle into her mouth |
| MARY | And out |
| MARY | We begin to fear we too are cursed |
| MARY | Our eyes close against our will |
| MARY | Time stands still within the palace but thunders on outwith |
| MARY | Who knew there could be so much time between eighteen and twenty |
| MARY | An icy frost has covered the fields |

| MARY | There will be no harvest |
| MARY | The skies are flaming forks of red |
| MARY | A sign of God's anger |
| MARY | // Knockes said |
| MARY | Your brother is burning witches |
| MARY | Old women no longer afraid to speak the truth are suddenly dangerous |
| MARY | Your chapel is attacked by militant Reformers |
| MARY | With a mob at their back |
| MARY | Your private chapel is sacrosanct |
| MARY | Built by your father |
| MARY | Decorated by your mother |
| MARY | Master Knockes is writing letters |
| MARY | Far and wide |
| MARY | Urging one and all to descend upon the city |
| MARY | To defend the attackers |
| MARY | John Knockes is always writing letters |
| MARY | The better part of his day is spent describing harlots and the Antichrist |
| KNOX | I call upon all of you who remember our most recent pledge in Ayr against the shameful sight of the mass being got up again in our once-blesst land |
| | To gather together in support of our two innocent brethren, who will be charged in Edinburgh |
| MARY | He is openly instructing them |
| MARY | // To assemble |
| KNOX | // To assemble ourselves in defence of our godly brothers this October Twenty-Fourth |

| | |
|---|---|
| MARY | He calls my people to assemble? |
| MARY | It is surely // treason |
| MARY | // Treason |
| MARY | No man shall summon my people to assemble without my permission or there will be sanctions, it is the law of the land |
| MARY | We have him |
| MARY | This time we have him |
| MARY | Maitland |
| MARY | // Maitland |
| MARY | Call my Privy Council, we will discipline this Reformer once and for all |
| MARY | Step together |
| MARY | As I should have done before |
| MARY | Step together |
| MARY | Let's see him cry for a change |
| MARY | Step step step |

# ROAAAAAAAAAR

| | |
|---|---|
| MAITLAND | Chatelherault<br>Argyle<br>Marischal<br>Ruthven<br>Glencairn<br>And your brother |
| MARY | Have you ever read, my lords, a more spiteful and treasonous letter? |
| MAITLAND | You must heartily repent that such a letter ever left your pen, Master Knockes |
| KNOX | To repent I must be aware of the offence |
| MAITLAND | That you did call the Queen's subjects to assemble |

KNOX          I am almost daily instructed by the Kirk's
              brethren to call the multitude to assemble for
              prayers and sermons, there is nothing
              unlawful in that, sir

MARY          This is no call to prayer, you have summoned
              my subjects without my command

KNOX          I was addressing Secretary Maitland, from
              whom I might expect a more educated
              argument

MARY          Rude rude rude

KNOX          Have you forgotten, my lords, who called the
              brethren against the Papist French?

MARY          Is he talking about my mother?

KNOX          And our hard-fought battles on that very hill
              behind you? Was that also unlawful?

MAITLAND      That was then, when our Queen was not in the
              country, but she is now

KNOX          The presence or absence of the Queen is
              irrelevant, I am ruled by God's plain
              speaking, what was lawful to me then is
              lawful now, and I see the flock in no less
              danger than at any time before

MARY          He is trifling with you, he admits he wrote the
              letter, is that not treason enough?

JAMES         Calling his flock to prayer is not the same
              thing as treason

MARY          Brother?

KNOX          But when we last confronted that danger it
              was in plain sight, on a battlefield, now it is
              hidden behind a visor, disguised as your ruler

MARY          You see how he confuses the truth with his
              opinion, and what of cruelty, he accuses me of
              cruelty, treason again, treason, I say

| | |
|---|---|
| KNOX | Am I to be damned before I am heard, my lords, are you not the Privy Council, before whom I am summoned to address? |
| MARY | He is guilty and he knows it |
| KNOX | Were we not once before in the power of the Papists? |
| LORDS | // Aye |
| MARY | No, brother, can you not see? |
| KNOX | And do we not remember their barbarous cruelty against our beloved sons and fathers |
| LORDS | // Aye |
| MARY | Can none of you see how he twists his words? |
| KNOX | And we know that these same pestilent Papists have so inflamed Her Grace, that she would murder our two brethren unjustly arrested and charged |
| BRETHREN | // Roaaaaaaarr |
| KNOX | Because it is Jesus Christ's enemies who have her confidence and they are dangerous counsellors |
| MARY | Now he accuses me of being murderous |
| BRETHREN | // Roaaaaaaarr |
| MARY | This is enough<br>I will have your judgement, lords |
| MARY | I will wait here |
| MAITLAND | John Knox has offended the Queen and is guilty, what say you? |
| LORD | I find him to be modest |
| LORD | He is plain and sensible |
| MARY | You are afraid of the crowd in the courtyard, speak the truth |

| | |
|---|---|
| LORD | I would not offend God by condemning an innocent man |
| LORD | I find him to have committed no offence |
| MAITLAND | He came here with a crowd in order to intimidate you |
| JAMES | Are you not satisfied that you control the Queen, Maitland, would you control us too? |
| MARY | Vote, vote, vote, I say |
| MAITLAND | All those who find John Knox to be guilty of treason, say Aye |
| LORD | No |
| LORD | No |
| LORD | No |
| LORD | No |
| MARY | Brother? |
| JAMES | God forbid that the lives of the faithful are ever again in the hands of the Papists |
| MARY | He feels my fear for my safe-keeping, in the rafters a draught blows through the opening door, a conspiracy of |
| LORD | It could be done now |
| LORD | If we had the nerve |
| LORD | The steel |
| LORD | The end might serve us right well |
| LORD | And our neighbour |
| MARY | Who's with me? |
| LORDS | … |
| MARY | Vote again, he is guilty of treason, as God is my witness |
| LORDS | … |

| | |
|---|---|
| MARY | Dismiss the mob and vote again |
| MAITLAND | Your Majesty |
| MARY | It became obvious that day how the men in this realm would betray me |
| LORD | You are free to go, Master Knockes |
| KNOX | God purge your heart, Madam, and preserve you from the counsel of flatterers |
| MARY | They failed to stand as one with the Crown so we are torn asunder, split in two warring tribes, as is Satan, and his / sister |
| JAMES | Sssister? |
| MARY | I am your Queen and you have betrayed me, leave me, leave me, let me be |

# CLICK

| | |
|---|---|
| BRETHREN | Roarrrrrrr |
| KNOX | There will be no dancing and fiddling this night |
| | . |
| MARY | The beginning then |
| MARY | That led to long |
| MARY | Long years of shrinking freedom |
| MARY | Capture in an English prison |
| MARY | And delivered us to our end |
| MARY | Mamaaaaaaaaaaaaaaaaaaaaaaaaaaaaa<br>Forgive me<br>I am not strong<br>I fall I fall<br>Help me<br>I cannot rise<br>Let your tender love claim me<br>Fold me into your warm embrace |

You gave me breath
But I am so unhappy
Alone
And the road ahead has never been darker
I long for sleep
Forgive me
I have nowhere to turn

MARY          // Uh hmm

MARY          Pity me pity me

MARY          // Marie

MARY          Abandonnée

MARY          // Uh hmm

MARY          Terrorisée

MARY          Mais tu es la reine, chérie

MARY          Je suis l'enfant

MARY          Et je suis toujours ta maman

MARY          But I don't know what to do

MARY          // Uh hmm

MARY          // Uh hmm

MARY          Or how to be

MARY          // Uhh hmm

MARY          // Uhh hmm

MARY          // Uhh hmm

MARY          Il était un petit navire

MARY          // The first berth to France then

MARY          The first step

MARY          As we stand on the dock

MARY          Your hand locked in mine

MARY          The future is unwritten, Marie

| | |
|---|---|
| MARY | But what does that mean? |
| MARY | You are five years old, be bold be courageous, you have been chosen by God in his infinite wisdom to carry the heart of your country in your soul |
| MARY | But I don't want to leave you |
| MARY | You're not leaving, petite, you are arriving |
| MARY | Il était un petit navire |
| MARY | But what if they ask me something I don't know |
| MARY | No one knows everything |
| MARY | I might refuse to go |
| MARY | Are you the Marie I know, are you the same Marie who will throw herself on to a pony and ride for half a day or more? |
| MARY | Qui n'avait ja-ja-jamais navigué |
| MARY | But what if? What if? |
| MARY | Let go my hand and walk to the ship |
| MARY | // Mmm mmm mmm mmm mmm |
| MARY | But I'm not ready |
| MARY | // Mmm mmm mmm mmm mmm |
| MARY | Glide from one moment to the next |
| MARY | What if I trip and fall? |
| MARY | God will not turn his back on you |
| MARY | Will he hear me? |
| MARY | Do well, think well, give thanks to God every day |
| MARY | Qui n'avait ja-ja-jamais navigué |
| MARY | Stand up |

| | |
|---|---|
| MARY | Straight back |
| MARY | Make the future your own |
| MARY | I don't seem to be able to put one foot in front of the other, Mama |
| MARY | Then fly, throw your heart over the space between here and the next place |
| MARY | Wait wait |
| MARY | You're never more alive than when you're afraid |
| MARY | ohé ohé |
| MARY | From above I see myself let go her hand and walk with steady footfalls on the wooden planks |
| MARY | // Click clack |
| MARY | // Click clack |
| MARY | // Click clack |
| MARY | // Click clack |
| MARY | // Click |
| MARY | Wait<br>Wait |
| MARY | // Uhh |
| MARY | I mean<br>At least we died with dignity<br>Didn't we? |
| MARY | // Chop |
| MARY | // Chop |

**www.nickhernbooks.co.uk**

 facebook.com/nickhernbooks

 twitter.com/nickhernbooks